lickin' the beaters

Low fat vegan desserts
illustrated by eight
faNtastic aRtists.

BY: SiUE MoffAt.

For all the vegan punk rockers

Lickin' The Beaters: Low Fat Vegan Desserts Illustrated by
Eight Fantastic Artists

ISBN: 978-1-60486-004-7
Library of Congress Control Number: 2007906932

Cover Illustration by Joe Ollman
Cover Design by John Yates

Published by:
PM Press
PO Box 23912
Oakland, CA 94623
www.pmpress.org

Printed by 1984 Printing, Oakland, CA on 100% recycled PCW, acid free paper with soy-based ink
www.1984printing.com

Distributed by AK Press
www.akpress.org

Be on the look out for two great feature films from Toronto: "End of the Year" by Ben Kukkee and "Grilled Cheese Sandwich" by Jonathan Culp. See these films, and I'll send you two yummy recipes that didn't make it into this book.

Acknowledgements

A warm thank you to my wonderful artists: Joe, Allyson, Brenda, Daryl, Five Seventeen, Missy, Zoe and especially Jonathan who kept pestering me to finish this book. Big thanks to my editors: Daryl, Five Seventeen, Joanne, Michele, Sarah D, Jonathan. Also Zoe, Charlotte and Five Seventeen for contributing heavenly concoctions. Gratitude to Jim, No Media Kings and Ben who always encouraged and supported me to Do It Myself! Malcom for providing me with tools to do it myself. Special thanks to Daryl and Five Seventeen who went above and beyond their illustrator duties and contributed to all the other aspects of production. Grateful thanks to mom, dad, Sarah K and everyone else who has encouraged me and showed interested during the 6 years it's taken to finish! Thanks to William at Marc Veilleux Imprimeur for answering **so** many questions and taking good care of me. And of course thanks to Craig, Ramsey, Amy, John, and PM Press for actually making the reprint happen. You would not be holding it in your hands without them! Cheers to *Soy, Not Oi* and *Raggedy Annarchy's Guide to Vegan Baking and the Universe* for being so influential. **Stikky** is the name of a great punk band – hence the continual tribute.

There are many groups and books out there that will help you along the vegan road. *How It All Vegan* and *The Garden Of Vegan* are good recipes and revolution cookbooks! www.govegan.net

Hello! Welcome to my cookbook!

I love desserts. I've always loved desserts and when I gave up meat, eggs and dairy I *still* loved desserts. In those first few months I craved rice crispie squares, gello and fudge. I thought that denying myself these luscious foods went hand in hand with animal rights and being healthy, because even the health food snacks were high in sugar, or contained animal products, or were just plain too *expensive*. But then it occurred to me, "Can't I make these myself? And why do yummy things have to be reserved as 'treats'?" By making desserts with little or no fat, whole flours, decreasing sugar and substituting dairy and eggs you can enjoy these wonderful foods without guilt and (within reason) whenever you wanted.

Eating is sometimes not an easy thing if you've chosen a vegan/healthful diet. How much fat is there? Does it contain animal products? Is it all natural? Is it expensive? People choosing a healthy lifestyle have to give things up. Staying away from eggs and dairy is a good idea (see page 93 on why you'd want to be a vegan) but what about cakes, puddings and pies? When was the last time you were encouraged to eat donuts, cheesecake or apple pie everyday? Or have a second helping? *Lickin' the Beaters* encourages "indulgent" behaviour with no apologies! Any guilt will instantly vanish when your body thanks you for feeding it a yummy healthy brownie!

In this book you will find many of the old favourites you used to pig out on and some new and interesting recipes that will satisfy your sweet tooth and your yearning for scrumptious desserts...not to mention keeping your wallet intact for fun things like icing bags and candy thermometers! Go crazy! Become a vegan baking machine!

 Note: Recipes contributed by the illustrators are NOT generally low fat and tend to be quite rich. They are *real* treats. These pages are marked with a little symbol to let you know.

Ask for this book at your local library! They will order it in for you!

Notes on Vegan Desserts

1. Buy as much as possible in bulk: less packaging and waste.

2. Nearly all these desserts and sweets require refrigeration because there isn't enough oil/fat to keep them from spoiling at room temperature. If your cake/pastry is fairly moist, take it out of the original pan after a couple of days and put it in a container or on a plate. A good rule of thumb — just about everything is safe in your fridge for a week. After that it's questionable.

3. There are only one or two cake recipes in here that call for sifted flour. I think sifting is overrated — who's got time?! However, it will help lighten your cakes if you find this to be a problem.

4. If you aren't into low fat baking simply replace the applesauce with oil or margarine. Not everyone is interested in eating desserts every day and some people are firm believers that all desserts should be sugary and greasy!

**This book is not a book for "dieters"! I don't encourage "diets" in the "let's eat as little as possible" sense. Just as every body type needs exercise, every body type needs a filling, wide variety of veggies, nuts, grains and fruit. Put away that scale, pull out your bicycle and make some vegan sticky buns!

Notes on Ingredients

Agar agar: This is a vegan gelatin that comes in powder, flake, and bar form. It's found at health food stores and Asian markets. I find the flake form easier to find so most of the recipes are made with that. Regular gelatin is made of cow hooves.

Chocolate chips: Semi-sweet chocolate chips are often free from diary products but they still contain sugar, which is most likely refined (see below). Dairy-free, unrefined chocolate chips are hard to come by and extremely expensive. Carob chips sometimes contain milk solids — check the ingredients.

Flour: Usually, you can use whatever flour you want in a recipe, though always stay away from bread or *hard* flour — this was never meant for delicate cakes or pastries. Look for the word *soft* in front of unbleached white or whole wheat flours. I have found that kamut and barley or kamut and spelt are really great and you can't tell it's not refined white flour. I've also used corn, oat, and brown rice with good results when mixed with whole wheat, spelt or kamut.

Ground flaxseed: an egg replacer found in healthfood stores. It should always be refrigerated as it becomes rancid quickly. You can grind your own seeds as well.

Margarine: Margarine often has whey (milk derivative) or gelatin in it. Keep an eye out for these ingredients. Unhydrogenated is best as hydrogenation changes the molecules of the fat and has been shown to cause cancer!

Molasses: Try to buy unsulfurized molasses. Most commercial molasses, raisins and other dried fruit use sulfur in processing. As with all chemicals, it's best to stay away from it. I suggest blackstrap because it has lots of vitamins. Don't use more than a 1/3 of cup though — it's bitter. The other types of molasses such as Fancy are sweeter and more like table syrup.

Peanut butter: Use natural peanut butter — free from hydrogenated oil, sugar and salt — you don't need that extra stuff!

Soymilk: You can use any kind of milk alternative — rice, soy, almond, grains etc. I usually use vanilla flavoured.

Sugar: The term *sugar* means any variety: unrefined (turbinado, demerara), "raw", or sucanat — it's all fair game. Sugar can be replaced in most recipes with maple syrup — just lessen the liquid in the recipe. *White Sugar* means turbinado style for strict vegans. (Regular white sugar is often refined using animal bones. Regular brown sugar is refined sugar with some molasses added.) Some recipes require a fine sugar. Use "raw" (a.k.a. organic) for this — it's as fine as regular refined sugar. *Brown sugar* means demerara style. Icing sugar is refined white sugar mixed with cornstarch, so it's also suspicious. Use maple syrup (look for the pure stuff!) in place of honey if your ethics extend to our friends the bees. You can experiment with rice syrup — it's just not cheap

OLD FAVOURITES

Ice Creams, Puddings & Toppings

NEW TASTY TREATS

Page

Fruity Stuff

Cakes & Donuts

BANANA BREAD — PERFECTO!

Banana breads can have up to a cup of oil in them. This one gives you more banana flavour instead. You could even replace the applesauce with another mashed banana.

3 c whole wheat flour
3 tsp baking powder
1 tsp baking soda
1/2 tsp each: cinnamon, nutmeg, cardamom
1/2 c pecan pieces
1 c maple syrup
3 very ripe bananas, mashed
1/2 c applesauce
approx. 1/4 c water

1. Preheat the oven to 350°.
2. Mix the flour, baking powder, baking soda, spices and pecans. Mix maple syrup, mashed bananas, applesauce and water.
3. Add wet to dry and add more applesauce/water as needed to make a batter that's thicker than pancake but a little thinner than cookie batter.
4. Put into a greased loaf pan and bake for 45-50 min.

BROWNIES & FROSTING

Easy, tasty and maybe even good for you!

1 c rice flour (or unbleached white)
1 c whole wheat flour
1/2 c carob powder (or cocoa)
1 1/2 tsp baking powder
1/4 tsp salt
3/4 c maple syrup
a little less than 1/4 c applesauce
1 tbsp canola oil
1 tsp vanilla
1 1/4 c water

1. Preheat the oven to 325°.
2. Mix the flours, carob, baking powder and salt.
3. Mix the maple syrup, applesauce, oil, vanilla and water.
4. Add wet to dry and bake 35 min. in an 8" or 9" greased pan.

FROSTING:
1/3 c carob chips
2 tbsp peanut butter
1/4 c water
2 tsp cornstarch mixed with a bit of water
1 tbsp sugar

1. Melt the chips, sugar and peanut butter in a double boiler (or one pot on top of a larger pot of boiling water). When it's melted add a 1/4 cup of water and stir out any lumps. Use more water if necessary. Add the cornstarch, stirring constantly, to thicken it a little.
2. Spread icing on the cake while warm — it will harden somewhat when it cools.

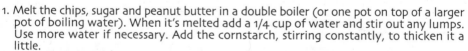

From Charlotte's Kitchen:
CHARLOTTE'S NEVER BEEN TO NEW YORK UNCHEESECAKE
Five Seventeen version

1 tub (8 oz) vegan creem cheeze, plain or with fruit (see page 50)
3/4 c soy yogurt (see page 49) (or soft silken tofu)
1 c firm tofu
3/4 c brown sugar
egg replacer equivalent to 2 eggs
1/4 c flour
1 tsp vanilla
pinch of salt
1 graham cracker crust (see page 40)
fresh fruit such as strawberries, mangoes, etc.

1. Preheat oven to 325°.
2. Blend all ingredients until smooth.
3. Pour mixture into graham cracker crust. Bake in oven for 50 min.
4. Allow to cool. Top with fresh fruit.

For Chocolate Marble Uncheesecake:
In saucepan melt 1 cup of chocolate chips. Mix melted chocolate into 1/2 of filling. Pour vanilla mixture onto crust then pour chocolate mixture on top in a zig-zag pattern. Use a spatula to mix, being careful not to over-stir or scrape the crust.

(Ed. note: You have not had vegan cheesecake so realistic until you've tried this recipe!)

CHOCOLATE DONUT HOLES

A note about raised, yeast donuts: Personally I prefer them but in a lot of shops the raised ones are fried in animal fat. I've made great vegan ones but they were fried. This cake kind still satisfies that donut urge.

3 c whole wheat flour
3/4 c sugar
1 tbsp baking powder
1/4 tsp salt
3 tbsp cocoa powder
1 c soymilk
1/4 c applesauce
oil

1. Mix flour with sugar, baking powder, salt and cocoa.
2. Mix milk with applesauce then stir into flour mixture.
3. Cover and refrigerate dough for about 30 min.
4. Preheat the oven to 350°. Take the dough and roll into balls.
5. Put a little oil in a bowl. Dip and coat your donut holes with oil and place on a greased cookie sheet.
6. Bake until they are done in the middle, about 10-15 min. Shake in a bag with icing sugar or fine sugar while still warm.

Who knows why people feel the need to deep fry cake. For **Spiced Donut Holes** you can substitute the cocoa for approximately two teaspoons of spices like cinnamon, nutmeg and allspice. You can also mix the sugar with cinnamon and coat the donuts with that.

FUDGE BROWNIES

At last! A low fat vegan fudge brownie recipe. They are hard to come by!

2 tbsp ground flaxseed mixed with 6 tbsp water (whip well with whisk!)
1/2 c applesauce or 1/4 c applesauce and 1/4 c oil
1/2 c soymilk
1 1/2 c maple syrup
2 tsp vanilla
2 3/4 c whole wheat or spelt flour
1/2 c cocoa
3/4 c chocolate chips (optional)

FROSTING:
1/4 c + 3 tbsp soymilk
4 tsp arrowroot or cornstarch
2 tbsp almond or cashew butter
4 tbsp cocoa
7 tbsp maple syrup

1. Preheat oven to 350°.
2. Whisk flax seed, applesauce, soymilk, maple syrup and vanilla then add the flour, cocoa and chocolate chips.
3. Let batter sit for 30 min. to thicken.
4. Pour into 9"x13" or 8"x8" greased baking pan. Bake for 25-35 min.

Frosting: Blend 3 tbsp of soymilk, cashew butter, cocoa and maple syrup until smooth. Mix the 1/4 c soymilk and cornstarch. Heat everything in a pot on medium low for 10 min., stirring occasionally as it thickens. Cool and spread onto cooled brownies.

PECAN STIKKY BUNS

These buns are best warm, but even if they're not, they will be gone in no time!

DOUGH:
1/2 c soymilk
1/4 c applesauce
4 tbsp brown sugar
2 tbsp turbinado sugar
1/4 tsp salt
2 tbsp yeast
1/2 c warm water mixed with 1 tsp sugar
2 tbsp soy yogurt (see page 49)(or just use soymilk)
2 tbsp ground flaxseed mixed w/ 6 tbsp water
2 c + extra soft whole wheat flour
2 c soft white flour

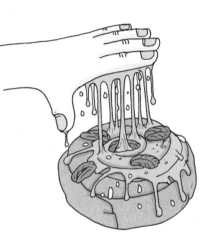

FILLING:
2 tbsp margarine
2 tbsp applesauce
1/2 c brown sugar
1/2 c chopped pecans
1/2 tsp cinnamon

TOPPING:
3 tbsp applesauce
4 1/2 tbsp brown sugar
3/4 c maple syrup
1/2 c chopped pecans
1 tbsp oil

1. For the dough: mix milk and apple sauce, stir in sugars and salt. In a separate bowl, mix yeast with warm water and a teaspoon of sugar. Let it get foamy (about 5 min.). Stir to dissolve. Stir soy yogurt, flaxseed mixture and milk into the yeast. Mix in 2 c of flour until blended. Stir in 2 more cups and knead until dough comes together. You may need to add a bit more flour to form a ball.
2. Flour your work surface and knead dough until smooth and elastic, adding more flour

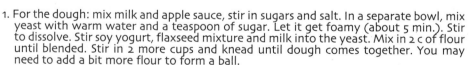

as needed. It will be very soft and a little stikky. Place into an oiled bowl, turn to coat, cover with a damp cloth and let rise until it doubles (about 1 1/2 hrs.)
3. Mix all of the filling ingredients together.
4. Mix the topping ingredients together except for the oil. Pour into a 9X13" pan.
5. Punch down dough and shape it into a ball. Roll the dough onto a floured surface forming a 24"x10" rectangle. Brush dough with oil and sprinkle evenly with filling. Starting on a long end, roll the dough jelly roll style. Cut cross wise to get about 15 slices, 1 1/2 inches each.
6. Put 1 tbsp oil on a sheet of waxed paper and place over your buns. This is to keep them from drying out as you let them rise again for 45 min.
7. Bake at 350° for about 30 min. Run a knife around the edges of the pan, place a cookie sheet on top, then invert the whole thing so the buns are on the cookie sheet. Separate and eat.

Try other nuts, no nuts, or use slivers of marzipan in the filling.

SOUR CREEM DONUT HOLES

2 cups flour
2/3 c sugar
1/2 tsp baking soda
1 1/2 tsp baking powder
pinch cinnamon
1/2 c vegan sour creem (see page 50)
3 tbsp ground flaxseed mixed with 6 tbsp water (whipped well with whisk!)
some oil

1. Sift flour with sugar, baking soda, baking powder and cinnamon.
   Mix in sour creem and flaxseed to form a dough. Try not to handle dough more than necessary.
2. Cover and refrigerate dough for about 30 min.
3. Preheat the oven to 350°. Take dough and roll into shapes of donut holes. Let them stand on a floured board for 10 min. Put a little oil in a bowl. Dip and coat donut holes with oil and place on a greased cookie sheet.
4. Bake until they are done in the middle, about 10-15 min. Shake in a bag with icing sugar, "raw" sugar or "raw" cinnamon sugar while still warm.

GINGERBREAD CAKE

Gingerbread cake is not as easy to find as it used to be — thank goodness it's so easy to make!

1 c whole wheat flour
1 c oat flour
1/2 c kamut flour
1 1/2 tsp baking soda
1 tsp cinnamon
1 tsp ginger
1/2 c sugar
1/2 c applesauce
1/4 c rice syrup
1/4 c maple syrup
1/3 c molasses
1 c hot water

1. Preheat oven to 350°.
2. Mix flours, baking soda, spices and sugar. Mix applesauce, rice syrup, maple syrup, molasses and hot water.
3. Mix wet into dry.
4. Bake in a greased 8"x12" pan for about 40 min.

Traditionally eaten with whipped (tofu!) creem, for an extra kick add about a 1/3 cup of chopped candied ginger to the batter.

From Zoe's Kitchen:
PINEAPPLE UPSIDE-DOWN CAKE

TOPPING:
15 oz can unsweetened pineapple pieces, juice drained and reserved
4 tsp corn starch
1/4 c sugar
1/4 c margarine
1/2 c water
zest of 1 lemon

CAKE:
1/4 c oil
1/2 c sugar
2/3 c water
1 1/4 c unbleached pastry flour
2 tsp baking powder
1 tsp ground cinnamon

1. Preheat oven to 350°. Grease a 7"cake pan and set aside.
   In a small bowl mix the reserved juice with the cornstarch until it forms a smooth paste. Put the paste in a saucepan with the sugar, margarine and water and stir over low heat until the sugar has dissolved. Bring to a boil and simmer for 2-3 min., until thickened. Set aside.
2. To make the cake: place oil, sugar and water in a small saucepan. Heat on medium heat until the sugar has dissolved. Remove from heat and allow to cool. Meanwhile sift the flour, baking powder, and cinnamon in a large bowl. Mix in the sugar mixture and beat well to form batter.
3. Place the pineapple pieces and lemon zest on the bottom of the cake pan. Pour 4 tablespoons of the pineapple syrup over the pineapple and lemon zest. Spoon the cake batter on top.
4. Bake for 35-40 minutes, until set. Invert on to a plate to let stand for 5 min. before removing the pan. Serve with the remaining syrup.

RICHER BROWNIES

These brownies are kind of in between the other recipes. Not quite fudgey, not quite cakey. They are dense and chewy. They also have a lot of sugar!

1 banana
1 c applesauce
1 c cocoa or 1/2 c cocoa and 1/2 c carob
1/8 tsp salt
1 1/2-2 c sugar
1 1/3 c flour
1/2 c chocolate or carob chips

1. Preheat the oven to 350°.
2. Mash the banana well, then add the applesauce and mix.
3. Mix cocoa, salt, sugar, and flour then add the banana/applesauce mixture.
4. Pour into an 8"x8" square greased baking dish. Bake for 35 min.

TRIFLE

This is probably the most time consuming recipe of the bunch. In the end, though, you'll have a fabulously gourmet vegan dessert that will amaze your friends!

CAKE:
1 1/2 c flour
3/4 c sugar
1/2 c cocoa
2 tsp baking powder
pinch salt
3/4 c milk
1/2 c applesauce
1/8-1/4 c soy yogurt (see page 49 or blended soft tofu)
1 1/2 tsp vanilla (or use the chocolate banana cake recipe in this book on page 55)

1 package of vegetarian gello, any flavour

2 1/2-3 cups of custard (cans of custard powder have instructions. Use soymilk instead of regular milk and voila! Or see **Theda Beehive Custard Cake** page 63)

1 c firm tofu, some maple syrup and soymilk

1-2 c raspberries

1. Preheat the oven to 325°. Combine all the dry ingredients for the cake and in a separate bowl combine all the wet. Then mix the two together and put into a glass or foil greased pie dish (8"). Bake about 45 min.
2. When the cake is baked and cooled, put into a bowl with a big enough bottom so that most of the cake is supported at the bottom (or else the cake will break in the middle and sag. Alternatively, if you happen to have a tall 8" or 9" round dish, like a soufflé dish, that would work well).
3. Make the veggie gello. Pour onto cake and chill according to the box.
4. Whip up the tofu with a few tablespoons of maple syrup. Add some soymilk if you need it smoother. This will be your whipped cream.
5. Next add the custard on top of the gello cake. Then sprinkle raspberries and dollop on the tofu whipped creem.

You can use your favourite white cake in place of the chocolate. The raspberries can be substituted for any fruit and you can substitute the gello with jam.

Candies

SWISH.
SCRAPE.

CHOCOLATE FUDGE

This is for real! Throw out all those awful recipes that use marshmallows, cream or evaporated milk.

1 1/2 c sugar
1 1/2 oz pure unsweetened chocolate
pinch of salt
1 c soymilk
2 tbsp margarine
1 tsp vanilla
1/2 c chopped nuts (optional)

1. Get a large pot. This is needed because the fudge bubbles quite a bit. Grease a small pan or other container.
2. Grease the sides of the pot and combine sugar, chocolate, salt and soymilk. Over medium heat, stir continually until the sugar dissolves and the mixture boils. Cook until 238° — soft ball stage (drop a little fudge into glass of cold water. It should form a ball and when you take the ball out it should flatten between your fingers.) *Do not stir* while it is boiling!
3. Take the pot off the heat and add margarine. Let cool to 110° or lukewarm. Add vanilla and beat vigorously. Toss in the nuts. It will become thick and start to lose its gloss (this means it is nearly ready to set).
4. Just before you think the fudge is going to firm up (it should take a few minutes of stirring) pour it into the pan. Chill for about 15 min.

Make marble fudge by melting some vegan peanut butter chocolate chips and then mixing in with a knife right after pouring the fudge into the pan.

For **Peanut Butter Fudge**: Omit chocolate and margarine. After cooling to 110°, add 3 tbsp peanut butter and continue as stated above.

For **Maple Fudge**: 1 c maple syrup, 1/2 c brown sugar, 1 1/2 c milk, 2 tbsp margarine, 1/2 c chopped nuts (optional). Same directions as for chocolate fudge.

For **Sour Cream Fudge**: 1 c vegan sour creem (or make your own! See page 50), 3/4 c sugar, 2 tbsp margarine, 1 tsp vanilla, 1/2 c chopped nuts. Same directions as for chocolate fudge.

If you stop cooking at 230° you will get amazing **Fudge Frosting**!

From Zoe's Kitchen:
PEANUT BRITTLE

2 1/2 c dry roasted peanuts
1 c sugar
1 c light corn syrup
1 tbsp baking soda
1 tbsp margarine

1. Grease a large baking pan. Set aside. Combine peanuts, sugar, corn syrup in a medium saucepan. Bring to a boil over medium heat, stirring constantly.
2. Insert candy thermometer. Continue boiling without stirring until temperature reaches 295°, about 6 min. When sugar begins to brown, stir in nuts gently to ensure even coating. Remove from heat and stir in the margarine and baking soda. The mixture will begin to foam up, so mix it quickly and pour into the prepared pan.
3. As soon as the candy is cool enough to handle, use your fingers to stretch the brittle as thinly as possible over the baking pan. Allow the brittle to cool completely for about 45 minutes and break it into bite size pieces. Store in a sealed container. Keeps for up to 2 weeks.

PEANUT BUTTER CUPS

I encourage using carob because it is much better for you and in this case it takes on quite a chocolatey taste.

1 c chocolate or carob chips
1 1/2 c peanut butter
3 tbsp soymilk (optional)
1/4 c icing sugar or regular sugar (optional)
1 tsp salt (optional)
cupcake papers, cut by half or quarter in height

1. Melt the chocolate or carob with 1/2 c peanut butter. (Do this in a double boiler: one pot with boiling water with your chocolate in a pot on top.) You can add 3 tbsp of soymilk for a more milk chocolate taste. Spread this mixture in the papers.
2. Place the paper in muffin tins. Leave some chocolate aside to put on top. Let cool for 20 min.
3. Melt the rest of the peanut butter and salt. (If it's the natural kind you might want to mix in the icing sugar to give the most authentic taste.)
4. Put the peanut butter into the chocolate paper cups. Leave enough space at the top of the paper for the chocolate cap. Set aside for 10 min.
5. Pour the rest of the chocolate on top of the peanut butter and set aside again for 20 min.
6. After all this work, scarf down 2 or 3!

Cookies & Bars

DATE BARS

Date squares make great last minute potluck dishes.

3 c chopped dates
1 c water
3 cup rolled oats
2 c whole wheat flour
3/4-1 c brown sugar
1 tsp baking powder
1/2 tsp salt
1 c applesauce

1. Preheat the oven to 350°.
2. Chop the dates as finely as possible. I find it easier and quicker to slice them. (Some people use scissors.) Put dates and water into a saucepan and bring to a boil. Let simmer for about 10 min. The mixture will be fairly smooth with some lumps.
3. Add more water if necessary.
4. Mix oats, flour, sugar, baking powder and salt. Add applesauce and mix until ingredients are crumbly.
5. Put half of the oat mixture into a large, greased rectangular pan. Spread date paste onto oats and then spread the last half of the oats onto the dates.
6. Bake 20-25 min.

If you use sweetened applesauce, reduce the amount of brown sugar. You can use any kind of fruit in place of dates and water. Apples, peaches, blueberries, cherries…

FIG NEUTRONS

This one's a toughie! My friends ask, "Why bother?" At one time I could argue about real fig newties being filled with gross things and not being vegan, but now there are healthy newtons on the market made with whole wheat flour and natural ingredients. They are expensive so if you've got little cash and extra time, try this recipe!

1 1/4 c whole wheat flour
1 1/4 c white flour
1/2 tsp baking soda
1/2 c applesauce
1 1/3 c sugar
1 tsp vanilla
3/4 lb figs (stems cut)
1/2+ c water
parchment paper

1. Mix flours and baking soda in large bowl.
2. Mix applesauce and 1 cup of sugar in a bowl. Add vanilla. Whip well with whisk!
3. Pour wet ingredients into the dry. Form a dough with an electric beater on "low". This can also be done in a food processor.
4. Divide the dough in half, wrap in plastic wrap and refrigerate for 30 min.
5. Chop figs in a processor and put them in a pot with 1/3 c sugar and water. Cook on medium heat, adding more water until a chunky paste is formed. Remove from heat and let cool.
6. This is the tricky part. Take parchment paper and sprinkle flour on it. Roll out one half of the dough as thin as possible on the paper. Try to get a 16"x8" rectangle. Cut length-wise into 2 strips (16"x4") Place half the figs evenly down the center of each strip lengthwise. Fold sides of dough over filling. Press edges together to seal. Repeat with remaining dough and filling. This difficult because the dough is *very* stikky. Flour everything repeatedly if needed.
7. Cut each long bar into two pieces crosswise. Transfer to a greased baking sheet, seam side down and put in fridge for 20 min.
8. Preheat oven to 375° and bake bars 16-18 min. Cut bars into 1" cookies. Transfer to wire rack to cool.

GINGERBREAD COOKIES

This recipe makes cookies upon cookies so there are lots to share with your friends. Don't be shocked at the 1/2 cup of oil. It may be the most you'll find in this book but when you compare how much flour is used, it's still a low fat recipe.

1/2 c oil or margarine
1 c sugar
2 tsp baking soda
1/4 tsp salt
1 tsp allspice, cinnamon, ginger
2/3 c apple juice
1 1/4 c unsulfurized molasses
7 c whole wheat flour

1. In a large bowl beat the margarine or oil, sugar, baking soda, salt and spices. Add liquid and molasses.
2. Stir in enough flour to make a dough. Wrap in plastic and chill for a couple of hours.
3. Preheat the oven to 350° and grease two cookies sheets.
4. Roll dough to about 1/4" thick. Cut into funny shapes. (I use a foot.)
5. Bake for 10-15 min., leaving a space between each cookie. Let cool on the cookie sheets for a few minutes before removing.

LINZERTORTE BARS

It's not a cake! It's not pie! It's the almonds that make this dessert yummy and different. Traditional recipes say to let sit for a couple days before eating.

3/4 c applesauce
1 c sugar
1 tsp grated lemon rind
1 1/4 c white flour
1 c ground almonds
1/2 tsp cinnamon
1/4 tsp cloves
pinch salt
2/3 c raspberry jam

1. Cream the applesauce, sugar and lemon rind.
2. Mix dry ingredients together, then slowly mix into the applesauce. Knead dough for a few minutes. Separate 1/4 of the dough and form both pieces into balls. Wrap the dough in wax paper and chill for about 2 hours.
3. Pat the larger dough ball into a greased rectangular pan. Chill for another 2 hours.
4. Preheat oven to 375°.
5. Spread jam on dough. Roll out small dough ball and cut into strips. Place on top in a crisscross manner.
6. Bake for 25 min. Fill holes with more jam if you wish.

LOW FAT CHOCOLATE CHIP COOKIES

3 c flour
2 tsp baking soda
1/4 tsp salt
1/2 tsp allspice
2/3 c chocolate or carob chips
1/2 c brown sugar (demerara)
1/2 c light sugar (turbinado, sucanat or "raw" sugar)
1/2 c wheat germ
2 tbsp oil
3/4+ c apple juice

1. Preheat the oven to 300°.
2. Combine flour, baking soda, salt and allspice. Stir in the chocolate chips and add the remaining ingredients in order, while mixing well.
3. Drop batter on greased cookie sheet, flattening somewhat. Leave about an inch between each cookie. Bake for approx. 15 min.

Low fat cookies are quite difficult because they often turn out rubbery. By letting them cool on racks, you can crisp them up a little bit. This recipe makes a great textured cookie. If you prefer your cookies very crunchy see the **Crunchy Cookie** recipe on page 69.

VEGAN RICE CRISPY SQUARES

This recipe is a lot of work, but the final product is very much like what you enjoyed as a kid. See page 73 for an alternate recipe which is quicker but tastes a lot different.

Make mock marshmallow first.

1 c "raw" sugar
3/4 c corn syrup
1 c hot water
2 tbsp agar agar flakes or 1 bar
3 tsp vanilla

1. Mix sugar, corn syrup and 1/2 c hot water. Bring to a boil but do not stir. Cook to 246°. (Firm Ball stage. Do the water test: get a glass of cold water. Drop a little mixture into water and it will form balls. Take a ball out of the water and if it doesn't flatten it's ready.)
2. Mix agar agar with 1/2 c hot water. Boil for one minute in a saucepan so that it becomes clear and thick. Stir the agar agar into the sugar mixture and pour into a blender with a whipping attachment (or mix with an electric mixer), whipping for about 10 min.
3. Add vanilla to mixture then pour into a corn starched 9"x5" pan. Chill for about an hour or use right away.

SQUARES:
6 c crisped rice cereal
1 tsp vanilla
3 tbsp margarine

1. Take a little more than half of the marshmallow and melt it if it's been chilled.
2. Add margarine and vanilla to the marshmallow. Mix and add 6 c of rice crispies. Press into a 9"x5" or larger greased pan. Chill for a few hours, or until firm.

Pies

PIES

Start with your crust and anything is possible!

1/2 c whole wheat flour
1/2 c white flour
4-6 tbsp cold water
2 tbsp oil or applesauce
2 tbsp sugar

1. Mix all ingredients together to form a dough. Wrap in plastic or wax paper and chill while you make the inside.
2. Roll out dough to fit your pie plate, then carefully press it into place. Poke a few times with a fork.

Apple pie: Make two dough recipes. Peel about 6 Granny Smith apples and slice thinly. Mix in 1/3 c sugar, 1 tbsp flour, 1 tsp cinnamon, 1/2 tsp nutmeg, 1/4 tsp ginger. Put coated fruit into the unbaked pie crust and place the other rolled out crust on top. Slice a few slits into the top so the whole thing doesn't explode!

Berry pie: Use 4 cups of any washed berries you want. Pit and slice cherries. Put fruit in an unbaked pie crust, sprinkle with 2 tbsp of cornstarch and approximately 1/4 c of maple syrup. You can make extra dough and cut into strips to lay on the top, or cover with foil.

Chocolate pie: Bake the pie crust first. 400° for approximately 10 min. First make the recipe for **Chocolate Pudding** (see page 44). Blend 1 c silken tofu, firm or soft, and slowly add the chocolate pudding. Add enough pudding so it's thick and tastes chocolatey. Put chocolate into the baked crust and chill 1-2 hours.

Coconut pie: See **Coconut Pudding** recipe on page 80.

Peach Crumble: Mix 3 tbsp of flour, 3 tbsp sugar and 1 tsp cinnamon. Toss with 3 c of peeled and sliced peaches. For the top mix 1/4 tsp nutmeg, 1/2 c brown sugar, 1/3 c flour, 1/3 c rolled oats and 2 tbsp applesauce. This mixture will be crumbly. Put the peaches in the unbaked pie crust and sprinkle on the topping.

3. Bake the pies at about 300-350 degrees for about 40 min. Small berry pies will require lower heat and shorter baking time. Apple pies require higher heat and up to 60 minutes of baking time. To see if your pie is finished baking insert a knife into a piece of the fruit. If the fruit is soft then the pie is baked enough. If the topping browns too fast put a piece of tin foil on top.

Mix and match! Try an apple crumble or add blueberries with your peaches! Impress the cute zinester around the corner!

BANANA CREEM PIE

Top with **Whip Creem** (see page 50) and you've got a luscious dessert you'll want to hide from the roommates.

4 bananas
1/2 c soy vanilla yogurt
2/3 c brown sugar
1 tbsp oil
2 tsp vanilla
2 tbsp agar agar
1/2 c soymilk
2 tsp cornstarch mixed with 1/4 c soymilk

Use regular crust (see page 36. Bake for approx. 10 min. at 400°) or try this **Coconut Crust**:
2 tbsp margarine
2 c shredded coconut

1. Heat oven to 300°.
2. Spread margarine on pie plate and sprinkle coconut evenly. Press into place.
3. Bake for 15-20 min. Cool.
4. Blend the bananas, soy yogurt, sugar, oil and vanilla.
5. Boil the soymilk and pour over agar agar. Simmer on medium low until dissolved.
6. Heat the banana mixture and add the cornstarch mix. Cook for 5-10 min. Take off heat and add soymilk/agar agar.
7. Pour into crust and chill until set.

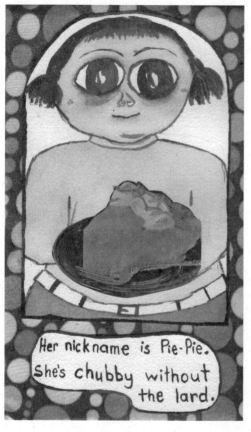

Her nickname is Pie-Pie. She's chubby without the lard.

LEMON MERINGUE PIE

Similar to diner pie. Another recipe to blow away an ignorant dessert denier.

COOKIE CRUST:
see graham crust on page 40. Use crushed vegan vanilla wafers instead of graham crackers

FILLING:
1/3 c cornstarch
1 1/4 c sugar
pinch salt
1 1/2 c boiling water
3 tsp of egg replacer mixed with 4 1/2 tbsp water
1/3 c freshly squeezed lemon juice
2 tsp grated lemon rind
1 tbsp margarine

MERINGUE:
12 tsp egg replacer mixed with 6 tbsp water
2 tsp agar agar mixed well with 4 tbsp boiling water
4-8 tbsp "raw" sugar
2 tsp vanilla (use clear if you want white meringue)

1. Preheat oven to 350°.
2. Mix cornstarch, sugar, salt and boiling water. Add egg replacer. Cook this mixture over medium heat until it thickens. Add lemon juice, rind and margarine. Pour into pie crust.
4. For the meringue, boil agar agar until dissolved and clear. Whip all ingredients with an electric mixer until it gets very thick and has incorporated some air. Spread on top of pie.
5. Bake for 15 minutes. Refrigerate until firm.

Try substituting chocolate grahams or ginger snaps in the crust. If you're budget conscious only use 1/2 meringue recipe and spread on a thin layer or distribute in patches

KEYLIMISH PIE

Really scrumptious with mock whip creem. Looks nice too!

3 c boiling water
1/4 c creamed coconut
3/4 c sugar
3 tbsp cornstarch
1/2 c lime juice
1 1/2 tsp grated lime rind
1 1/2 tbsp agar agar

Graham crust: Mix about 2 cups of graham cracker crumbs with some applesauce until it can be pressed into an pie pan. Bake for approximately 12 min. at 350°. Once I added way too much applesauce and got a doughy mush but it still worked out ok. You can also use this crust for other pies and bars. (Bake about 5 min. if you don't need a pre-baked crust.)

1. Pour boiling water onto coconut and dissolve. Set aside approximately 1/2 c of this mixture and heat the rest in a pot with sugar.
2. Mix cornstarch with the 1/2 cup coconut milk and add to the pot.
3. Pour 1/2 c boiling water onto agar agar and dissolve over low heat.
4. When the coconut mixture is thick, take off heat. Add lime juice, rind. and the agar mixture.
5. Pour into pie shell and chill for about 2 hours.

Ice Creams, Puddings & Toppings

BANANA SPLITS

MY TONGUE
LIKES
BANANAS

NOT MILK MEN

This is a perfect dish to eat with a person you think is very neat.

2 tbsp margarine
1 tbsp sugar
1 tsp cornstarch
1 tbsp soymilk
1/2 tsp vanilla
about 1/2 c of any berries
1/4 c of water mixed with 2 tsp cornstarch
a small container of vegan ice cream, or other (see page 44)
2 bananas
some **chocolate sauce** or:
2 tbsp soymilk, 1 1/2 tbsp cocoa, 2 tbsp maple syrup, 1 tbsp cashew butter (or peanut).

1. Melt the margarine, mix in sugar. Mix the cornstarch into the milk and add vanilla. Add the milk mixture into you pan. Heat until thick. This is your **caramel sauce**.
2. Put the berries in a saucepan and heat with water/cornstarch mixture. Heat until thick. This will be your **berry sauce**.
3. To make your chocolate sauce mix up the ingredients in a pan on low/med. heat.
4. Let sauces cool.
5. Put each banana in a separate dish and split them down the center. Put three scoops of ice cream on each one. Then drizzle the sauces — one for each scoop of ice cream.

Tah-da! You can use bottled sauces or jam but it's cheaper to make your own since you don't need that much.

BREAD PUDDING

Both these desserts are really great on their own… Don't believe anyone who says bread pudding can't be good without eggs!

3 c soymilk
2 tbsp lemon juice
1/2 c + 2 tbsp brown sugar
2 tbsp margarine
2 tbsp ground flaxseed mixed with 6 tbsp water (whipped well with whisk!)
2 tsp vanilla
3 c bread crumbs

1. Mix soymilk with lemon juice and let stand 5 min. Preheat the oven to 350°.
3. Mix soymilk, brown sugar, flaxseed and vanilla.
3. Pour soymilk mixture over the bread crumbs and mix well.
4. Put into greased 2-quart casserole dish and bake about 1 hour.

For **Cherry Peary Bread Pudding**: Add 1/3 c dried cherries, 2 medium pears, diced and replace the vanilla with 1 tsp almond extract.

Try bread pudding with this topping:

Pineapple Cloud
10 oz extra firm silken tofu (or firm regular tofu)
19 oz can crushed pineapple, juice reserved
1 tsp vanilla
maple syrup to taste

1. Start with the tofu, blend, then add the pineapple and other ingredients. If needed, add pineapple juice. Keep the texture like a thick pudding.

CHOCOLATE PUDDING

1/3 c cocoa
2/3 c of sugar (or less if using sweetened cocoa)
pinch of salt
1/3 c cornstarch
3 c soymilk
1-3 tbsp margarine
2 tsp vanilla

1. Mix cocoa, sugar, salt and cornstarch. Add the soymilk while whipping constantly with a whisk.
2. Bring to boil over medium heat, while still whipping. Lower heat and cover. Simmer 5-10 min.
3. Remove from heat. Stir in margarine and vanilla. Chill.

Remember gello **Pudding Popsicles**? Well you can make your own! Use this recipe, use 2 tbsp of cornstarch instead of 1/3 c, and pour into popsicle trays, or ice cube trays with toothpicks!

CHOCOLATE MOUSSE

What a great dessert! Think of all that calcium and protein you're getting while you satisfy your sweet tooth!

1 c soft/silken tofu
1/4 c chocolate or carob chips
1/4 c maple syrup
2 tsp vanilla

1. Blend the tofu until it's smooth and creamy. Silken tofu works best for this but plain soft tofu is fine as well.
2. Melt chips with a tiny bit of water or soymilk. Add chips, maple syrup and vanilla to tofu. Mix it well and chill.

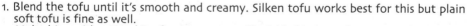

CREAMY RICE PUDDING

Wow! Do you remember the rice pudding you'd get from the school cafeteria? This tastes exactly like it... From the kitchen of Sue Culp.

1/2 c short grain rice (sweet brown stikky rice is great)
1 c boiling water
1/3 c sugar
1 tsp cornstarch
pinch salt
5 c soymilk
1 tbsp cinnamon
1/4 c raisins (optional)
1 tsp vanilla

1. Put rice and boiling water in a large pot. Bring to boil and simmer 15 min. (or less – do not let rice soak up all the water, as it will stick and burn!)
2. Combine sugar, cornstarch and salt. Whisk in a cup of soymilk.
3. Add sugar mixture and remaining milk to pot. Add cinnamon and raisins. Bring to a boil.
4. Cover and reduce heat until barely simmering. Cook for 1 1/2-2 hours, stirring occasionally.
5. Stir in vanilla.

ICE CREAMS

If you don't have an ice cream maker, you can still fulfill your craving. The trick is to freeze the ingredients in a metal pan and whisk occasionally until firm and creamy *or* freeze until solid then pop into a processor for a few quick blends and freeze until firm again. Either way, it takes almost a full day. Once the ice cream has been in the freezer for a while it will need to *ripen*. This is when you stick it in the fridge to soften a little before serving it. Generally, if you find your ice cream too hard, you should ripen it. Always store in a tightly covered container. See the **Orange Dreamsicle Shake** recipe for tips on using your ice cream maker (page 88). If you don't mind the bad stuff, substitute 1 cup non-dairy whipped topping for tofu in all the recipes.

Cardamom Pistachio

Melt 1/3 c sugar with 1/2 c water and boil 5 min. Chill to room temperature.
Stir in 1 c non-dairy whipped topping, 3/4 c soymilk, 3 tbsp chopped pistachio nuts, 1/4 tsp ground cardamom. Freeze or use ice cream maker. This one's cheating a bit. The whipped topping is full of bad stuff like hydrogenated coconut oil, but this is an excellent ice cream.

Chocolate

Heat 3/4 c sugar with a little soymilk to make a syrup. Then chill to room temperature.

Mix 1/3 block of silken firm tofu with about 2 cups of soymilk, 1/4 c cocoa powder and the syrup. Freeze or use ice cream maker.

Chocolate Peanut Butter

Heat 1 c sugar with a little soymilk to make a syrup. Then chill to room temperature.
Blend 1 c firm silken tofu, 1/3 cup cocoa powder, 1/3 cup peanut butter, 1 tsp vanilla, about 2 1/2 cup soymilk. Freeze or use ice cream maker.

Strawberry

Make the syrup in the vanilla recipe and chill.
Blend 1 pint of strawberries with 1/3 block of firm silken tofu, about 2 cups of soymilk (Feel daring? Use strawberry flavoured soymilk), 1 tbsp lemon juice, the syrup and 1/4 tsp vanilla. Freeze or use ice cream maker.

Vanilla

Heat 3/4 c sugar with a little soymilk to make a syrup. Then chill to room temperature.
Mix 1/3 block of silken firm tofu with about 2 cups of soymilk or soy yogurt, 1/3 c yogurt cheeze, the syrup, 1 tbsp vanilla. Freeze or use ice cream maker.

SMALL TWIN SUNDAES

Once, while my twin second cousins visited my mom's house, I helped them make sundaes. Now my mother has to make sure she's always got a supply of ice cream and toppings.

2 scoops chocolate ice cream
2 tbsp raspberry jam
2 tbsp blueberries
1/4 c whip creem
2 black cherries
Sprinkles

1. Put one scoop each into glass or dish. Top with jam, blueberries, whipcreem and cherry. Sprinkle liberally with sprinkles.

VANILLA PUDDING

Just when you think you're a chocoholic, you melt away with thick and creamy vanilla pudding.

4 c soymilk
1/4 c cornstarch
1/2 c brown sugar
pinch of salt
3 tsp vanilla

1. Put 3 1/2 c of the soymilk in a pot. Heat some water in a larger pot than this one.
2. Heat soymilk almost to a boil. Mix the cornstarch with the remaining 1/2 c soymilk and then add a little heated soymilk. Pour this into the boiling soymilk and stir well.
3. Place the pot of soymilk into the larger pot of boiling water which acts as a double boiler. cook the mixture for 10 min.
4. Remove soymilk mixture from heat. Mix in sugar and salt until dissolved. Stir in vanilla and let cool for a few minutes.

VEGAN YOGURT

2 litres of soy/rice milk (8 cups)
a 500 g tub of vegan yogurt
OR a package of yogurt starter OR good dairy yogurt
A baking/candy thermometer and funnel if you have them

1. Buy a small tub of plain or vanilla vegan yogurt avail-
   able at better health food stores. This will ensure an
   absolute vegan recipe. If you can't get the vegan kind
   or don't want to spend the money, get a cheap package of yogurt starter. This is made from milk so your
   yogurt won't be truly vegan but it'll be close enough.
2. Use two 700ml clean glass jars (like from pasta sauce
   or applesauce) or a really big jar, and boil water in a
   big pot that will fit the jars. At the same time you're
   boiling this water pour the soymilk — 6-8 cups into
   another pot and heat to boil. When the water boils
   place jars in the pot upside down. They tend to flip
   on their sides so move them about as they boil. Add
   clean lids, the clean spoon you want to use to stir and
   measure your yogurt with, a cooking thermometer if

   you've got one, and a funnel if you have one to make pouring easier. Boil (sterilize)
   everything for two minutes. Sterilizing is important in order to ward off bad bacteria!
   Let soymilk boil for 30 seconds, stirring constantly. Pour the milk into the jars and put
   the lids on.
3. Cool down — this can be done in the fridge or on the counter. It takes about an
   hour. You want to cool the milk until it's 110°. If you don't have a thermometer the
   temperature is right when you put the glass against your wrist and it doesn't burn.
   Stir the yogurt or yogurt starter in the jars — 2 tbsp of yogurt to each jar (4 tbsp
   work with 6-8 cups milk)
4. Incubation — your work is nearly done. Put the jars in the oven and turn to 150° for
   3 min., then turn off the heat. (If using gas, just put the jars in and the pilot light will
   do the job.) Let jars sit undisturbed for about 6 hours. I have found I need to turn on
   the heat (of the electric oven) for a couple minutes more at about 2 1/2 hr intervals
   because my oven loses heat. You need to try and keep a constant 104° so your
   soymilk will change to yogurt. After 4 hours you may want to check. Turn the jar on

it's side and if comes clean away in a big solid or large chunks, it's ready. If you let it sit too long it will separate into curds and whey and you don't want that. If your yogurt is pink, fizzy or slimy throw it all out, wash, resterilize and try again.

In terms of the soymilk to use, I have tried rice milk, brand name soymilks and soymilk from Chinatown. They all work. I usually go with the Chinese kind because it's cheap. The additional sugar takes away the sour taste. When using special unsweetened soymilks you need to add about a tablespoon of sugar while it's boiling. To keep your yogurt nice and thick add sweeteners, salt, vanilla and other goodies as you eat it. You can make a new batch using this batch. Use 1 tablespoon to each 1 cup of soymilk.

WHIP CREEM

10 oz (1 1/4 cup) firm tofu (silken is best)
4 tbsp sugar, honey or maple syrup
2 tbsp lemon juice
1 tsp vanilla extract
soymilk as needed

1. Put all in a blender or food processor, whip well. Add some soymilk if the mixture is too thick.

YOGURT CREEM CHEEZE/SOUR CREEM

After you've made vegan soy yogurt, take some and put it in a fine mesh sieve, cheese cloth, or a clean cotton cloth. Set the sieve on a cup or bowl, cover and refrigerate. Or tie the cloth so that it hangs over your sink. In a few hours most of the liquid will have dripped out of the yogurt and you'll be left with this cheeze. Add some lemon juice and a little soy milk and you'll get sour creem. Add a little bit of sugar/maple syrup and lemon juice and put on bagels or make into creem cheeze icing by adding icing sugar.

Cakes & Quickbreads

"I'd rather be eating cake!"

SAVE TIME SAVE WORK SAVE MONEY

baked treats

BANANA COCONUT CAKE

Bananas are really great in baked goods, they can replace all of the oil. The topping is adapted from the **Oatmeal Spice Cake with Coconut Topping** (see page 60).

1/2 c whole wheat flour
1/2 c brown rice flour
1/2 c corn flour
1 tsp baking powder
1/3 c coconut
3 very ripe bananas
1/4 c brown sugar
1/3 c white sugar
1 tsp vanilla

TOPPING: 1 tbsp oil
1/2 c coconut
1/3 c chopped pecans or
walnuts
3 tbsp soymilk

1. Preheat oven to 350°.
2. Mix flours, baking powder and coconut.
3. Mash bananas and add sugar and vanilla.
4. Mix wet and dry ingredients together. Spread into a greased 8"x8" square pan. Bake 25-30 min.
5. Combine oil, coconut, nuts and soymilk to make the topping.
6. Cool cake slightly, spread on the topping. Brown the top under the broiler (about 550° for 2-3 min. on most ovens. Be careful not to burn it.)

BERRY BUTTERMILK QUICK BREAD

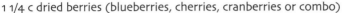

Little nuggets of fruit stud this moist, not-too-sweet, quick bread.

1 1/4 c dried berries (blueberries, cherries, cranberries or combo)
1/2 c water
2 c spelt flour
1 c kamut flour
3 tbsp sugar
3 tsp baking powder
1 c vanilla soymilk + 1 tbsp lemon juice
2 tbsp applesauce
1/2 c maple syrup
1/2 tsp vanilla

1. Preheat oven to 350°. Combine lemon juice and soymilk. Put the berries and water in a pot, bring to a boil, simmer about 5 min., then cool.
2. Mix flours and baking powder.
3. Mix sugar, soymilk, applesauce, maple syrup and vanilla.
4. Drain the berries and reserve 1/3 cup of liquid. Make a well in the dry ingredients and add the wet ingredients. Mix until moistened and add the 1/3 cup of reserved liquid if necessary. Fold in the drained berries.
5. Bake for about 35 min.

BLACK BANANA CAKE

This was concocted at the spur of the moment one New Year's eve with my friend Ben. It's the anti-social banana cake...

4 or 5 completely black (but not rotting!) bananas
2 tsp vanilla
1/4 c oil
2 c flour
1 tsp baking powder
3/4 c sugar
19 oz can of pineapple rings

1. Preheat oven to 350°.
2. Mash bananas and add vanilla and oil. Mix well.
3. In a separate bowl mix flour, baking powder and sugar together.
4. Grease two round cake tins and place pineapple rings at the bottom.
5. Mix the wet and dry ingredients together and pour evenly into the two tins.
6. Bake for about 1/2 hour or until toothpick comes out clean, though the top might look wet.
7. Stack the cakes.

CHOCO-BANANA CAKE

A twist on the popular and close to the heart **Soy, Not Oi** recipe.

1 1/2 c flour (white or whole wheat)
1 c sugar
3 tbsp cocoa or carob
1 tsp baking soda
pinch of salt
1 tsp vanilla
1 mashed banana
approx. 3/4 c water

1. Preheat the oven to 350°.
2. Mix flour, sugar, cocoa, baking soda and salt.
3. Mix vanilla, banana and water.
4. Mix the wet into the dry ingredients.
5. Pour batter into greased cake pan and bake 30-40 min.

OPTIONAL ICING:
Use the frosting in the **Brownies and Frosting** recipe (page 14) or the **Fudge Brownie** frosting recipe (page 17).

From Charlotte's Kitchen: CHOCOLATE TURTLE TRUFFLE TORTE

1 c flour
1 c oats
1/4 c fructose or sugar
3/4 lb margarine
3/4 c brown sugar
1 c pecans, toasted
1 lb semi sweet chocolate chopped
3/4 c soymilk or almond milk

1. Preheat oven to 350°. In a medium bowl mix flour, oats and fructose. Cut 1/4 lb margarine into small cubes. Mix into dry ingredients with a fork until crumby. Press mixture firmly and evenly into the bottom of a springform pan.
2. Bake for 15 min. or until slightly browned, then cool.
3. To make a caramel sauce, melt 1/4 lb margarine in a small saucepan. Add brown sugar and stir constantly until the mixture is smooth and melted. Slowly stir in 1/4 c soymilk. Stir until smooth and shiny. Pour caramel over cooled crust.
4. Sprinkle pecans over caramel. Chill for approximately 20-25 min. or until the caramel thickens.
5. In a double boiler (or small pot over a bigger pot of boiling water) place remaining 1/4 lb margarine and chocolate. Pour in remaining 1/2 c of soymilk and stir until smooth.
6. Pour chocolate mixture over caramel crust in a spiral motion, working inwards so as not to disturb the pecans too much. Tap bottom of pan on counter to settle the chocolate.
7. Chill to set, about 2 hours. This is a VERY rich dessert, so it can be cut into 16 small pieces.

CRANBERRY BREAD

Adapted from my cousin Christie's recipe. You can whip this up quick when you're too lazy to make an elaborate dessert.

2 c whole wheat flour
2 tsp baking powder
1 c sugar
1/2 tsp baking soda
1/4 tsp salt
2 tbsp oil or applesauce
1 c orange or apple juice
1 1/2 c cranberries

1. Preheat the oven to 350°. Mix flour, baking powder, sugar, baking soda and salt in a large bowl.
2. Make a little well in the dry ingredients and pour juice and applesauce or oil into it. Mix well.
3. Fold in cranberries. Pour into a greased loaf pan (8"x4"). Bake about 50 min. or until toothpick comes out clean from the middle of your loaf.

DESSERT SCONES

1 c less 2 tbsp soymilk
1 tbsp lemon juice
1 1/4 c white flour
1 1/4 c whole wheat flour
2 tbsp baking powder
pinch of salt
1/4 c sugar
1/2 c mini chocolate chips (or any kind of chips/chocolate, chopped a bit)
3 tbsp applesauce
1 tbsp oil
1/3 c jam (raspberry or cherry is good)

1. Mix soymilk with lemon juice and let stand for 5 min. (this will be the buttermilk).
2. Preheat oven to 375°.
3. Measure flour by spooning it into a measuring cup. Combine flour with baking powder, salt and sugar. Add chocolate chips.
4. Mix in buttermilk, applesauce and oil with a pastry cutter until mixture just holds together. Do not over mix. Add more flour if you can't get a dough ball that can be put onto a floured surface.
5. Shape dough into a 9"x9" square. Add more flour if you need to keep if from sticking. Cut into 8 triangles.
6. Put them on a greased baking pan and make a dent in each one using a floured spoon. Fill the dents with jam.
7. Bake for about 12 min. and let cool 5 min. before you devour them.

Forget donuts for breakfast. For **Cranberry Scones with Lemon Glaze**: substitute chocolate chips with dried cranberries, omit the jam and drizzle with lemon glaze: 1/4 c icing sugar, 1 tsp lemon zest, 1 tsp lemon juice, 1/2 tsp soymilk.

FIGGY CARROT LOAF

A tasty combination and good for you, too. Eat as a snack or dessert.

1 c chopped figs
1/4 c juice from canned pineapple
1 c whole wheat flour
1 1/2 tsp baking powder
1 tsp baking soda
1 1/2 tsp cinnamon
3/4 c crushed pineapple
just over 1/3 c brown sugar
1 tsp vanilla
1 c grated carrot

1. Preheat oven to 350°.
2. Combine figs and juice in blender.
3. Mix the rest of the ingredients in a bowl, then add the fig puree.
4. Pour into a greased loaf pan and bake for 50 min.

POPPYSEED PINEAPPLE LOAF

A not-too-sweet quick bread that is good with apple butter or a glass of carob soymilk.

2 c whole wheat flour
1/2 c sugar
3 tbsp poppy seeds
1 tsp baking powder
1 tsp baking soda
8 oz can crushed pineapple, with juice
1/3 c soymilk
1 tsp almond extract
1 tsp vanilla

1. Preheat oven to 350°. Mix flour, sugar, poppy seeds, baking powder and baking soda.
2. Mix the pineapple, juice, soymilk, vanilla and almond extract. Stir into dry ingredients until moist. Pour into greased loaf pan. Bake for about 40 min. Let cool for 10 min. before removing from pan.

OATMEAL SPICE CAKE WITH COCONUT TOPPING

This is adapted from the fabulous **Raggedy Annarachy's Guide to Vegan Baking and the Universe**. It's very moist and hard to stop eating!

1 1/2 c flour
1 c quick cooking oats
1/2 c brown sugar
1/2 c sugar
1 3/4 tsp baking soda
2 tsp cinnamon
1/2 tsp nutmeg
1/2 c applesauce
3/4 c water
1 ripe banana
2 tbsp molasses

TOPPING:
2 tbsp margarine
2/3 c brown sugar
1/2 c coconut
5 tbsp soymilk

1. Preheat oven to 350°.
2. In a processor (or with a bowl and electric beater) mix cake ingredients well, then on high beat for a few minutes. I'm sure you can do it without the devices, just mix with a whisk for a while.
3. Pour into 8"x8" greased pan and bake for about 40 min.
4. For the topping, melt ingredients and spread over cake while still warm. Put the cake under the broiler (about 550° on most ranges) for 2-3 min. until brown.

SPICED PUMPKIN BREAD

2 c whole wheat flour
1/2 c brown sugar
1 1/2 tsp baking powder
1 tsp baking soda
1/2 c canned pumpkin
2 tsp pumpkin pie spice
3/4 c orange or apple juice
1/3 c chopped pecans (optional)

1. Mix flour, sugar, baking powder, baking soda and nuts.
2. In a separate bowl mix the remaining ingredients.
3. Preheat oven to 350°. Mix wet and dry ingredients together until moist. Pour into a greased loaf pan and bake for about 40 min. Let sit for 10 min. before taking it out of the pan.

Can you tell that I am crazy about orange coloured vegetables? You can try substituting canned pumpkin in place of applesauce or bananas in other cakes and bars for interesting flavours.

SUGAR PLUM COFFEE CAKE

Fairies with gluten allergies absolutely love this recipe!

1 banana, mashed
1/4 c maple syrup
3 c mixed wheat free flours (get creative!)
3/4 c + 2 tbsp brown sugar
1 tsp cinnamon
1 tsp nutmeg
1/2 tsp allspice
1 1/4 c soymilk
1 tbsp oil
8 plums, chopped

1. Preheat oven to 375°.
2. Mix the banana and maple syrup. Mix the flour with 3/4 c sugar and spices.
3. Mix all together to form crumbs. Reserve 3/4 of this mixture.
4. Next add the soymilk and oil to make a batter. Pour into a bundt pan or 8"x8" pan.
5. Mix the plums with 2 tbsp sugar and drop onto the top of the cake. Add the reserved crumb mix. Bake 50 min.

From Charlotte's Kitchen:
THEDA BEEHIVE CUSTARD CAKE

1 pkg vegan puff pastry (approx 400 gr)
2 tbsp margarine

TOPPING:
1 c sugar
1 c margarine
1/4 cup soymilk
1 c sliced almonds

CUSTARD FILLING:
2 cans coconut milk (approx 800ml)
1 1/4 c soy milk
1/3 c cornstarch
2-3 tbsp agar agar powder
2/3 c sugar

SQUEAK.
SQUEAK.

1. Roll pastry flat into four even rounds. Carefully place pastry in layers in a springform pan basting with margarine between each layer.
2. For the topping, melt sugar in double boiler, slowly adding margarine and soymilk. Stir constantly to keep things smooth.
3. For the topping, mix the sugar, margarine and soymilk. While still hot, pour topping over unbaked pastry. Sprinkle almonds evenly over the surface. (NOTE: Place a cookie sheet under the springform pan to catch any leaks.) Follow instructions for baking pastry.
4. After cooking, allow to cool. Cut pastry in half, making a top and bottom layer. Cut top layer into eight serving size sections. Cut top layer ONLY. Replace bottom layer of pastry into springform pan.
5. In a medium saucepan mix all the custard ingredients using a hand blender or a whisk. Bring the mixture to a boil over medium heat, stirring constantly. Turn the heat to low and continue to cook, still stirring, until the mixture thickens. After it thickens beat with a hand blender or whisk to make sure it's smooth. Carefully pour custard into the springform pan.
6. Place top layer (cut in eight) on top of custard. Allow to set for one hour in the fridge.

STRAWBERRY BANANA UPSIDE-DOWN CAKE

This is a very healthy cake. Make sure the bananas are very ripe, or they will become hard and dry instead of soft and gooey. Inspired by a little café in Columbia, MO.

2 heaping cups (approx. 1 lb) strawberries
2 ripe bananas
2 tbsp maple syrup
1/2 c white flour
1/2 c oat flour
1/2 c whole wheat flour
1/2 c sugar
1 tsp baking powder
1/2 c applesauce
3/4 c water

1. Preheat oven to 350°.
2. Chop strawberries and bananas. Place them at the bottom of an 8"x8" greased pan. Drizzle with maple syrup.
3. Mix flours with sugar and baking powder, add applesauce and water. Pour evenly over the fruit.
4. Bake for about 50 min.

TOTOES

There's a Caribbean bakery in Kensington Market that makes the best baked goods. This recipe emulates one of them.

3 c spelt flour
1 c brown sugar
1 1/2 c unsweetened coconut
1/2 tsp allspice
1/2 tsp cinnamon
3 tsp baking powder
1/2 c soymilk
1 tsp baking soda
1/3 c unsulfurized molasses
1/3 c + 2 tbsp maple syrup
2 tbsp ground flaxseed mixed with 6 tbsp water
1/2 c applesauce

1. Preheat oven to 325°.
2. Mix flour, sugar, coconut, spices and baking powder.
3. Dissolve baking soda in soymilk. Mix in molasses, flaxseed and applesauce.
4. Mix wet ingredients into dry and pour into a greased rectangular pan. (These can also be dropped onto a cookie sheet. Reduce baking time.)
5. Bake for 45 min. They're ready when a toothpick comes out clean. Cut into squares.

Cookies, Pies & Squares

BLUEBERRY CHERRY CRISP

When the cherries and blueberries are on sale in the summer, I make tons of this. I also buy extra berries and freeze them for winter crisp.

1 lb cherries
1/2 c rolled oats
1/2 c flour
applesauce
1 tsp cinnamon
margarine (optional)
1 pint of blueberries
maple syrup
1 tbsp cornstarch

1. Pit the cherries. This will take some time.
2. Preheat the oven to 350°.
3. Mix rolled oats, flour and cinnamon with applesauce and a little water if necessary until you get a crumbly mixture. You can also add a little margarine.
4. Put the cherries and blueberries into a big casserole dish. Add some maple syrup — you don't need more than a 1/4 cup. Sprinkle cornstarch on top. Then sprinkle the crumb mixture. Bake for about 20 min.

CHERRY DELIGHT

Originally from my mom, this recipe is full of prepackaged nasty stuff. But gosh does it ever taste good! ;)

1 package light vegan creem cheese (or make 10 oz of your own! See page 50)
1 litre tub of light non-dairy whipped topping
1 c icing sugar
4 c graham cracker crumbs
1/2 c sugar
1/3 c margarine, melted
1/3 c maple syrup
1/3 c applesauce
19oz can cherry pie filling *OR:*
3 c fresh/frozen cherries
3/4 c juice (1/3 c if using frozen berries)
1/4 c sugar
2 tbsp cornstarch

1. Preheat oven to 350°.
2. Mix sugar with graham cracker crumbs. Add syrup, margarine and applesauce to crumbs, mixing well. Pat down into a 9"x13" (or a little smaller) greased pan and bake 10 min.
3. With an electric mixer beat the cream cheeze a little, then add non-dairy whipped topping and icing sugar.
4. Spread the cream cheese mixture onto the crust. Chill overnight.
5. Pour cherry filling on top *or:*
6. Heat cherries in a pot adding sugar and most of the juice. Mix the left over juice with 2 tbsp of cornstarch. When the cherries are bubbling pour in this mixture, stirring well. Pour over crust and chill.

CRUNCHY COOKIES

These cookies differ from the other chocolate chip recipe in this book in that the amount of sugar makes them crunchy.

2/3 c flour
3/4 c brown sugar
1/4 c coconut
1/4 c chopped pecans
1 tsp baking powder
1/8 tsp salt
1/4-1/2 c chocolate or carob chips
1/3 c applesauce
1 tsp vanilla

1. Preheat oven to 350°.
2. Mix flour, sugar, coconut, pecans, baking powder and salt. Mix vanilla into applesauce. Mix applesauce into dry ingredients to form a dough.
3. Put dough balls on a greased cookie pan and press down flat as much as possible. Bake 10-15 min. and cool on a wire rack.

You could substitute peanut butter for applesauce and get a whole new flavour.

FROZEN BANANA PEANUT BUTTER PIE

Very simple but heavenly — whoooo.

about 1 1/2 c wheat and barley "nuts" cereal
maple syrup or applesauce
4–6 large bananas, peeled and frozen
3 tbsp maple syrup
2 tbsp lemon juice
1 c peanut butter

1. Grind the cereal in a blender until it is as fine as graham cracker crumbs. Mix with some maple syrup or applesauce in a bowl and press into the bottom of a pie tin to form a crust. For this recipe you require a pre-baked pie crust so bake at 350° for 10 min.
2. Put bananas in blender and add the maple syrup and lemon juice. Blend it up adding the peanut butter. If you use natural peanut butter you may want to add more maple syrup.
3. Put banana mixture into pie crust and freeze. Eat frozen.

This can be put into a glass or metal pan *without* the crust and eaten as ice cream!

WHIR.

WHIRRR.

WHIRR.

MAPLE OAT BARS

These bars have a really strong maple taste that is wonderful.

1/3 c applesauce
1 c maple syrup
2 c quick cooking rolled oats
1/2 c wheat germ

1. Preheat oven to 350°. Over medium heat, boil the applesauce and maple syrup together for a few minutes.
2. Remove from heat and stir in oats and wheat germ. Spread into a greased 8" pan. Bake for about 20 min.
3. Cool and cut.

Only use *real* maple syrup. The table syrups just don't cut it. In the U.S. the most common type of real maple syrup is Amber, while in Canada it's grade B medium. Therefore, in the States maple syrup doesn't have a very strong maple flavour. If you like intense maple flavour (like me) look for a grade other than Amber.

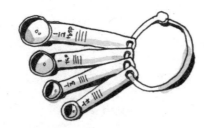

MAPLE PUMPKIN COOKIES

I just adore pumpkin in baked goods. Linus would be proud!

2 c whole wheat flour
1/4 c oat flour (or kamut, spelt, etc)
1 tsp baking soda
1 tsp cinnamon
1/4 tsp nutmeg
pinch salt
1/4 c margarine
1/2 c brown sugar
1/3 c white sugar
1 tbsp ground flaxseed mixed with 3 tbsp water
3/4 c mashed pumpkin
6 tbsp maple syrup

1. Preheat oven to 350°.
2. Mix flour, baking soda, cinnamon, nutmeg and salt
   together.
3. Cream sugar and margarine. Add flax
   mixture, pumpkin and maple syrup.
4. Gradually stir flour into wet
   mixture.
5. Drop large tablespoons of
   batter onto greased
   cookie sheet
   and bake for
   about 20 min.
   or until edges
   are brown.
   Cool on racks.

SCOOP.

CLANK.

RICE CRISPY THANG

i was raised on rice crispie squares... now, marshmallows are against my morals.

My friend Lisa remarked they remind her of a certain peanut butter and chocolate flavoured candy bar/cereal on the market.

1/4 c sugar
3/4 c corn syrup
1 c peanut butter
5-6 c crisped rice cereal
1/2 c chocolate or carob chips
(optional)

1. Heat sugar and corn syrup over medium heat until bubbly. Remove and add peanut butter and cereal. Mix and spread into a 9"x13" greased pan or similar.
2. Melt chips in a double boiler then drizzle on the squares.
3. Refrigerate until cool.

RHUBARB CRUNCH

I'm not one for rhubarb, but when it's around you have to use it, right? This is simple and quite good.

4 c chopped rhubarb
1 3/4 c sugar
1/4 c flour

TOPPING:
1 c oats
1/2 c flour
pinch of cardamom
2 tbsp applesauce
2 tbsp maple syrup

1. Preheat oven to 450°.
2. Chop fresh or frozen rhubarb. In a bowl, mix it with the sugar and 1/4 c flour. Put this mix in a 2 quart casserole dish.
3. Mix oats, flour and cardamom. Add applesauce and maple syrup. If you have a pastry cutter use this to crumb the mixture. A fork is ok too.
4. Put the topping onto the rhubarb and bake for 10 min. Turn down the temperature to 350° and bake another 35-40 min.

SPRINGERLES

When I was younger, my Aunt Cathy used to make these every Christmas. They are strange and I adore them. They are very dense and taste like licorice. You either love them or hate them.

1 1/8 c "raw" sugar
egg replacer equivalent to 2 eggs
2 c white flour
1/2 tsp baking powder
1/4 tsp anise oil

1. If you can't find a "raw" sugar and don't want to use refined, you'll have to melt the turbinado some way - possibly by adding a little water to it. Beat the sugar and egg replacer for *half an hour* (yes that's right!) with an electric mixer. Add anise oil.

2. Mix flour with baking powder. Slowly add to wet mixture and knead until stiff. Roll to 1/2" thickness and use cookie cutter to cut into shapes (I use a pig). Put them on a floured board and store in a cool room overnight (!)

3. Bake at 325° for 12-15 min. They will mostly stay white.

SWEET POTATO PIE

This is as good as pumpkin pie and more of a treat because it's not so common .

just over 1 lb sweet potatoes (2 c cooked and mashed)
1 tbsp oil
3/4-1 c soymilk
3/4 c brown sugar
2 tbsp molasses
1/4 c cornstarch
1/2 tsp nutmeg
1/2 tsp ginger
1/4 tsp cloves
1 tsp cinnamon
wheat and barley "nuts" cereal pie crust (grind cereal and make like graham cracker crust — see page 40)

1. Preheat the oven to 425°.
2. Mix mashed potato with oil, soymilk, sugar, molasses, cornstarch and spices. Pour into pie crust.
3. Bake for 10 min. then reduce heat to 350° and bake 45 min. more until filling is firm in middle.

Puddings & Candies

APPLE TAPIOCA

Nice and cozy when it's warm. After being in the fridge for a few hours it makes a great gello substitute for those vegan potluck picnics!

1/2 c minute tapioca
1/4 tsp salt
3 c apples, peeled and sliced
1 c brown sugar
1/3 tsp nutmeg
1 tsp cinnamon
2 tsp lemon juice

1. Cook tapioca, salt and 4 cups of hot water in a double boiler (or cook in a pot sitting on top of a bigger pot with boiling water.) Cook for 15 min. or until tapioca is clear. Stir frequently.
2. Preheat the oven to 350°.
3. Put apples in greased baking dish. Cover with sugar mixed with spices and lemon juice. Pour tapioca over this and bake for 45 min.

APPLE RICE PUDDING

Is this healthy rice pudding or what? Eat when recovering from a hangover! Sprinkle some cinnamon on the top for an extra kick.

2 tbsp margarine
2 apples, chopped
1/4 tsp cinnamon
1/4 tsp nutmeg
2 c cooked brown rice
1 c soymilk
1/3 c maple syrup
1/3 c wheat germ

1. In a pot, heat margarine, spices and apples. Add rice, milk and maple syrup. Heat until bubbly but not boiling. Reduce heat and simmer, stirring occasionally for about 15 min. If pudding isn't thick enough, add a few tsps of cornstarch or arrowroot mixed with a little water.
2. Put wheat germ in a dry frying pan and toast until brown. Sprinkle over pudding.

DATE BALLS

This doesn't sound like much but dates are so amazing! When you get a sugar craving eat this, or just plain dates. They are so sweet and your taste buds and body will thank you.

3 c chopped dates
3/4-1 c water
some coconut

1. Boil dates in water for about 10 min. until they become a thick paste.
2. Cool the dates and then form into balls and roll into coconut.

COCONUT PUDDING

3 c coconut milk
4 tbsp arrowroot or cornstarch
4 tbsp sugar
1/4 c shredded coconut
1 tsp cardamom
1/8 to 1/4 tsp cloves

1. Mix arrowroot into a little of the coconut milk.
2. Mix all in a saucepan. Heat over medium heat until thick. Stir often and do not boil.
3. When thick pour into bowl and chill for about an hour.

You can turn this into coconut cream pie using agar agar. Reduce cornstarch to 3 tbsp and use either 2 tbsp or one bar, broken up. Boil with 1/2 c water until it turns into a clear, smooth, gelatin like substance. Mix it with the thickened pudding and pour into a pie crust.

This is a special treat. Coconut is one of the few fruit/vegetables which are high in saturated fat. There are, however, a few companies that make lower fat coconut milks, which tend to be more expensive. You might try experimenting by using coconut water/juice and soymilk mixed together instead.

HALVAH - YOUR VERY OWN

1 c sesame seeds
1/2 c tahini (optional)
2 tbsp honey or maple syrup
1 tsp vanilla

1. Grind sesame seeds into a nut butter. I wasn't able to do this — my processor only cut the seeds in halves. If your processor can do this you won't need the tahini.
2. Put seeds into a bowl and add tahini, honey and vanilla.
3. Put the stikky mass into the smallest container you have, lined with wax paper — just so the halva isn't thicker than one inch.
4. Chill and cut into cubes.

This amazing candy is usually made with egg whites. You can add a tablespoon of cocoa if you want. You can marble it by not mixing well.

PERSIMMON PUDDING

6 very ripe persimmons
2 c soymilk
2 tsp vanilla
8 tbsp maple syrup
2 tbsp cornstarch mixed in 1/2 c soymilk

1. Scoop out flesh of the persimmons an place in a blender/processor.
2. Blend persimmons and add 2 cup soymilk, vanilla, maple syrup and cornstarch mixture.
3. Simmer on the stove until it thickens.
4. Chill.

While visiting The Ranch in Missouri, I was scandalized to find they let all their precious persimmons fall to the ground and rot. "Those are persimmons!" I declared, "You could sell them for 50 cents or a dollar each!" I don't think they believed me...

PBBC PUDDING

2 very ripe bananas
1/4 c peanut butter
2 tbsp cocoa, heaping
3 tbsp maple syrup
some vanilla soymilk

1. Blend all ingredients, adding enough soymilk to make a thick pudding. Use more
   syrup if you like it sweeter.
2. Chill or eat right away.

Comfort food doesn't get any quicker or delicious. You can get fancy and pour it into a
pie shell for **PBBC Pie**. Arrange sliced bananas on top.

PUMPKIN PUDDING

2 c cooked mashed pumpkin
1/2 c soymilk
3 tbsp maple syrup
2 tsp cinnamon
1/4 tsp nutmeg
1 tbsp finely ground almonds (or just use flour)

1. Preheat oven to 350°.
2. Blend everything and pour into baking dish.
   Bake for 50 min. or less.

Makes two medium size servings or one big one
just for you!

RICE MILK

1 c cooked brown rice
2 1/2 c water
2 tsp vanilla

1. Put rice into a food processor or blender. Blend, adding a little water at a time. If it looks like your processor is at its limit, pour out the milk part into a jar and keep the rice sediment in your processor as you add the rest of the water. The trick is to blend the rice until it's smooth, having as little sediment as possible.
2. Pour milk into a jar or container of some kind, using a fine mesh sieve to collect about half of rice sediment as you're doing it. Before each time you use the milk give the jar a few shakes. Store in fridge. Lasts a week or more.

This milk isn't close enough to soy or regular rice milk to be used in cereal or a pudding-based dessert because it's not thick enough, but it can be used in baked goods. What's great is that it costs pennies.

SWEET POTATO "SOUFFLÉ"

4 lb sweet potatoes (about 4 medium)
1/2 c soymilk
1/4 c margarine or applesauce
1/2 c brown sugar
1 tsp cinnamon

1. Dice potatoes and put in a pot with soymilk and extra water to cover.
2. Bring to a boil then reduce heat and cover. Simmer for 15-20 min.
3. Drain potatoes and reserve liquid. Put potatoes in a food processor.
4. Add margarine or applesauce, sugar and cinnamon. Blend well, adding cooking liquid to thin if necessary.
5. If you happen to have vegan mini marshmallows, sprinkle on top and broil for a minute to toast them.

I'm a big fan of sweet potatoes. For dinner or dessert they taste heavenly. What other dessert will give you so much Vitamin A?

Fruity Stuff

LUSCIOUS SALADS AND DESSERTS
...right at your finger tips!

Simply open can and dump into bowl!

BAKED APPLES

4 apples (pick a variety that holds it
shape like Granny Smith or Spy)
1/4 c dried cranberries or cherries
2 tbsp marzipan (almond paste)
1 tbsp ground hazelnuts (filberts)
1 tbsp slivered almonds
dash of apple juice

1. Preheat oven to 350°.
2. Core apples and peel if desired. Mix berries, marzipan
   and nuts together.
3. Fill the cored apples with the cranberry/almond
   mixture and then pour a tiny bit of apple juice into
   the core.
4. Wrap in foil and bake for 40-60 min.

Inspired by a recipe from an old German punk rock penpal.

From Zoe's Kitchen:
BANANA FRITTERS

1 1/2 c flour
1 t baking powder
1/4 tsp baking soda
3/4 cups water
4 firm bananas
5 c veg oil for frying

1. Combine 1 c flour with baking powder, baking soda and salt. Gradually add water and
   beat until smooth.
2. Cut each banana crosswise into 3 pieces — 12 pieces altogether. Coat bananas with
   remaining flour (1/2 cup) and heat the oil in a large skillet. Dip banana pieces in flour
   mixture, coating well. Cook 4-6 pieces at a time until golden brown, about 3-5 min.
   Instead of deep frying you can also fry them the same as you would pancakes.
3. Drain on paper towels. Serve with vegan ice cream. Yummy!!!!!

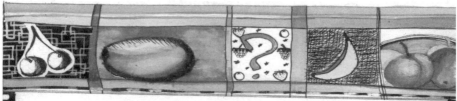

FRESH FRUIT AND TASTY TOPPING

1 c coconut
1/2 c dates
1/4 c finely ground almonds
4 cups of fruit — cherries, mangoes, peaches, blueberries, whatever your heart desires
2 tbsp maple syrup
1/2-1 tsp nutmeg

1. Grind dates, coconut and almonds together in blender or processor. The dates will cause quite a noise and possibly bounce your appliance around so keep a hand on it! It will be crumbly when you're done.
3. Cut up the fruit, place it in bowl or casserole dish, add maple syrup, sprinkle with nutmeg and then add topping. Mix around well.

Simple as that! Fresh fruit with an interesting twist. Eat great big bowls in the summer with a tofu BBQ!

MANGO PEACH DESSERT SOUP

3 peaches, roughly chopped
2 smallish mangoes, roughly chopped
1 tsp grated fresh ginger
1/4 c sugar (or less)
2 c white grape juice
2 tbsp lemon juice

1. Blend or process everything until smooth. Start with the fruit first and add juice little by little.
2. Put into a bowl and chill for an hour. Garnish with peach slices and a little bit of that yogurt you made. (Page 49)

A very light dessert good for when you're finished at the vegan buffet!

Milk gives me the creeps.
I'll take my creemsicle
without the cream please.

ORANGE DREAMSICLE SHAKE

3 c soy yogurt (page 49)(or use half soymilk, half vegan ice cream. Pages 46 and 47)
3 tbsp frozen orange juice concentrate
1/2 c sugar (use more or less to taste)
3 tsp vanilla
1 or 2 tbsp oil
pinch of salt

1. Combine all in a blender.

You can make frozen yogurt out of this, too. It's easy:

Freeze all ingredients in your ice cream maker. I bought a used hand crank machine for $5 with French instructions so I just guessed. Pour your mixture into the bucket, leaving about an inch at the top. Crank it relatively slow until it gets to a consistency of soft serve or fruit ices — not scoop ice cream. Store it in the freezer. This will harden so you'll need to thaw it a bit before you try and scoop it out. *Or:* Put into ice cube trays and freeze, then blend when you're ready to eat it. *Or:* Pour into popsicle trays.

Blend other whole fruits (a cup or more) instead of the orange juice concentrate to get interesting flavours. Freeze first if making frogurt.

PINK SNOW DRINK

ice cubes
2/3 c frozen coconut milk
1/2 c strawberries (about 7)
1/3 c grapefruit sorbet
2/3 c vanilla soymilk
1 tbsp maple syrup

1. Blend all ingredients.
2. Drink with a smile.

I often squander good desserts to myself. This concoction was *so* good I had to share it with everyone in the house!

STIKKY RICE AND MANGO

3 mangoes
3 cups cooked *stikky* or *sweet* or *glutinous* rice
1 c coconut milk (lower fat if you've got it)
1/4 tsp salt
4 tbsp sugar

1. Chill your mangoes.
2. Combine stikky rice and coconut milk in pot and cook on medium heat about 5 min.
3. Stir in sugar and salt. Cover and simmer for 2 min.
4. Peel and slice your mangoes.
5. Serve rice warm with cool mangoes.

Really yummy, and with only a small amount of sugar. Fully satisfying!

About the Artists

Allyson Mitchell is a maximalist artist working predominantly in sculpture, installation and film. Since 1997, Mitchell has been melding feminism and pop culture to play with contemporary ideas about sexuality, autobiography, and the body, largely through the use of reclaimed textile and abandoned craft. She has performed extensively with Pretty Porky and Pissed Off, a fat activist troupe, as well as published both writing and music. Check out her work at: allysonmitchell.com

Daryl Vocat is an artist living and working in Toronto. His work is greatly influenced by his experiences in the Boy Scouts as well as the imagery and teachings from Boy Scout manuals. Daryl's background is in printmaking, with an emphasis on intaglio and screen printing, although he dabbles in video and photography once in a while. "In my illustrations I wanted to demonstrate some of the joys of eating and the friendships that can go along with being in the kitchen with someone. Since food is such an integral part of all of our lives why not celebrate it. Yay for dessert!" darylvocat.com

Missy Kulik is one crafty lady. For over 15 years she's been a self-publisher, zinester, and comic artist. She studied graphic design, and when she's not applying those skills to her job in the art department of a major balloon company, she sews, knits, bakes, studies trapeze, and plays with Nilla, her cat. And when she's not doing any of that, she's making illustrations for magazines, or working on record covers, or drawing comics for local papers in Athens, Georgia. missykulik.com

Five Seventeen draws pictures of his cat Mr. Sniffy Rifkin and some people like them. Jean Clutha (a.k.a "the round cat") doesn't seem to care. His real name is Five Seventeen. Some other stuff can be found at: mymeanmagpie.com

Brenda Goldstein is an activist and filmmaker extraordinaire who hosts midnight screenings in her backyard. She wields a mean wallpaper roller and bikes around breaking hearts with her orange helmet. An hour older than Siue Moffat, Brenda's love of nostalgic images and the *Twilight Zone* come out in her artwork.

Jonathan Culp is the author and illustrator of "Cine-VHS", an international guide to making collage films with two VCRs. You can order it — and check out his many zines, recordings and movies, including the feature comedy "Grilled Cheese Sandwich" — at satanmacnuggit.com.

Joe Ollmann is often sighted lurching about the streets of Montréal pretending he understands some of what is being said to him. He is the author of three books: *Chewing on Tinfoil, The Big Book of Wag!* and *This Will All End in Tears,* all ostensibly "funny books" but mostly consisting of bug-eyed, bucktoothed characters enacting various depressing aspects of the misanthropic author's world view. wagpress.net

Zoe Dodd moved to Toronto in 1997 from Whitehorse, Yukon. After travelling around Europe, she learned some vegan cooking basics which sent her on the road to recovery from the junk food vegetarian diet. Now her sweet tooth is filled by creating tasty vegan treats and once a month she cooks amazing dinners for Punk Movie Night. Zoe is also a whiz in sewing, crafting, weaving and belly dancing. She's into punk and hardcore music, a member of the Fat Girl Skinny Boy Alliance and the Tiger Bicycle Gang. <zoe_dodd@hotmail.com>

About the Author

Siue Moffat is a dessert lover like no other who went vegetarian at 14. She occupies her time cooking, baking, making short films and fanzines, stressing about the state of the world and looking for film archiving work. Her second cookbook of vegan chocolate and candy will also be published by PM Press in 2008. You can keep up to date at dairyfreedesserts.com.

ARTIST INDEX

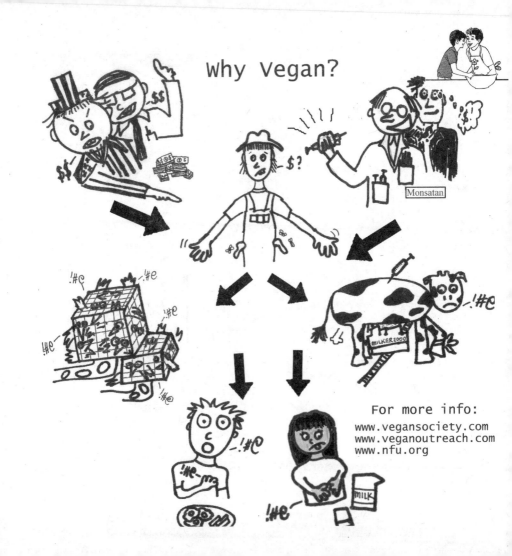

INDEX